A Golden Beginning Reader

Turtles

BY BERTIE ANN STEWART
AND GORDON E. BURKS

Illustrated by William Hutchinson
M. Vere De Vault, Educational Consultant

GOLDEN PRESS NEW YORK

Introduction

A Golden Beginning Reader

The Science Books in this series are easy-to-read and designed to satisfy the child's natural curiosity about the world in which he lives.

Each book contains factual information, presented with simplicity and imagination. The text and the illustrations work together to bring the child both pleasure and greater comprehension of the subject.

Parents and teachers will welcome this additional source of self-help information for young readers. With the stimulation of these Golden Readers, boys and girls can grow in their ability to read, in their understanding of science, and in their enjoyment of good books.

M. Vere DeVault
Professor of Education,
University of Wisconsin

1969 Edition
© Copyright 1962 by Western Publishing Company, Inc. All rights reserved, including the right of reproduction in whole or in part in any form. Printed in the U.S.A. Published by Golden Press, a Division of Western Publishing Company, Inc.

Library of Congress Catalogue Card Number: 62-12871

Turtles are four-legged reptiles.
They have been on earth
for millions of years.

Turtles lived on earth
long ago with the dinosaurs,
largest of all land animals.

The last dinosaur died
millions of years ago.
But turtles still live on.

Turtles live in many places.
Loggerheads live in the sea.

Box turtles live on land.

Gopher turtles dig holes in the soil,
then go to sleep inside.

Sliders live in rivers and ponds.

Map turtles, too, live in ponds,
and in marshes and streams.

Tiny spotted turtles swim
in fresh-water lakes.

Long-necked chicken turtles
dwell in ditches and ponds.

Pretty painted turtles are
the most common of all.
They sun themselves in swamps,
ditches, ponds, and slow streams.

Some turtles grow
to be very large.
The leatherback,
the largest sea turtle,
grows up to eight feet long.
It can weigh as much
as a small car.

The giant Galapagos tortoise,
the largest land turtle,
grows to about half the length
of the leatherback.
It can weigh up to five hundred pounds.
Galapagos tortoises live
for a long time.
Some of them have lived
for almost two hundred years.

Some turtles are very small.
The Muhlenberg turtle,
at home in or out of water,
never grows longer
than four inches.

The tortoise-shell turtle,
one of the smaller sea turtles,
grows to about thirty-five inches.

Its shiny spotted shell is used
to make jewelry and other ornaments.

Like most female reptiles,
all female turtles lay eggs,
usually from six to sixteen of them.
Sea turtles lay even more.

Most turtles bury their eggs
in loose earth,
or in sun-warmed sand.

Female sea turtles swim
to shore to lay their eggs.
They drag themselves slowly
up the beach and bury the eggs
in the sand where the water
cannot reach them.

When they are finished,
they go back to the sea.

Female turtles do not sit
on their eggs.
The eggs are hatched
by the heat of the sun.

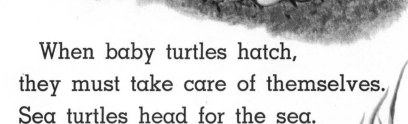

When baby turtles hatch,
they must take care of themselves.
Sea turtles head for the sea.

Land turtles stay on land.
All of them look for food.

Turtles eat many things.
Fresh-water snappers
feed on dead fish
and water plants.

Wood turtles eat fruit,
berries, and tiny animals.

Sea turtles eat seaweed
and sea animals such as
shrimps, crabs, clams, and fish.

Land turtles like snails,
worms, insects, and plants.

Turtles have no teeth.
But most have strong jaws and claws.

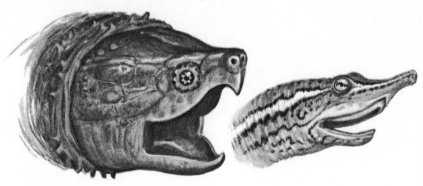

They use their jaws
to crush and tear their food.

The alligator snapper
stays on the muddy bottom
of its pond or stream.

It opens its mouth wide,
and wiggles a long pink ridge
on its tongue to attract fish.

Some turtles are very fierce.
Beware of the long-necked
soft-shelled turtles.

With their long necks,
they reach out to snap at
anything that comes near.

Some turtles are very shy.
The gentle Blanding's turtle
makes a very good pet.

It is found in the waters
and marshes of northeastern
United States.

All turtles have shells.
The one on top is called
the *carapace*.

The bottom one is called
the *plastron*.

The carapace of land turtles
is usually higher than
that of water turtles.

Land turtles use their shells
for protection.

When danger is present,
they draw head, tail, and legs
under the carapace.

Some water turtles protect their heads in a different way.

The side-necked turtle bends its very long neck to one side, and tucks its head under the edge of its shell.

Musk turtles and mud turtles
give off strong smells
to protect themselves.
These turtles smell so bad
that their enemies stay away.

Many turtles make good pets.
They are easy to take care of.
You can keep a pet turtle
in a bowl of water.
Put a rock in the bowl
for the turtle to climb on.
Pet turtles should be fed bits
of meat and fish, and very small
pieces of lettuce.

If you treat your turtle well,
it will live a long time.